WINNING DEALS IN HEELS

TOP WOMEN REAL ESTATE INVESTORS
SHARE STORIES OF OVERCOMING OBSTACLES
& ACHIEVING SUCCESS

NANCY WALLACE-LAABS

WINNING DEALS IN HEELS

TOP WOMEN REAL ESTATE INVESTORS
SHARE STORIES OF OVERCOMING OBSTACLES
& ACHIEVING SUCCESS

NANCY WALLACE-LAABS

Featuring:

KRISTIN GERST	SUE ABRAMS
AMY SAYRE	SUSAN TIERNEY
SANDRA J. NESBITT	MISSI LOU WILSON
JAMIE WOOLEY BURLESON	SHENOAH GROVE
LOLITA SHERIOW	BELKIS GUIFARRO

Winning Deals in Heels/Nancy Wallace-Laabs. -- 1st ed.
ISBN 978-1-946694-34-8

Royalties from the Retail Sales of
"Winning Deals in Heels" are donated to
Hope's Door New Beginning Center

Hope's Door New Beginning Center is a non-profit organization that is dedicated to building lives without violence in our community. We help individuals and families escape and heal from domestic abuse, dating abuse and family violence through our free trauma-informed services. Our community educators enhance the community's capacity to recognize and respond to abuse through free educational programming to schools and organizations, while our certified BIPP facilitators help individuals who have exhibited controlling or abusive behaviors in the past achieve healthy and non-violent conflict resolution skills.

You can learn more about Hope's Door New Beginning Center by visiting hdnbc.org.

DEDICATION

To my husband, Brian
– For your unwavering support of my dreams

To my daughter, Kelcie
– My heart and my WHY

To my friends, Zac and Heidi
– For your inspiration and guidance

To all the contributors
– Thank you

To all the future women real estate investors
– Good luck!

TABLE OF CONTENTS

INTRODUCTION

Since I was a child, I knew I wanted to write a book. About what, I was never sure, but I would not have dreamed in a million years that it would be about women real estate investors.

Over the last several years, I've met so many women who want to get into this business, and they always ask, "What is the most important thing I need to learn to succeed as a woman real estate investor?"

I've thought about this question a lot; it's the same question I had when I started my own real estate journey. Even though I've come up with a lot of great answers, I never felt I could truly pinpoint the *most important*, even wondering "Is there a Most Important?"

Surely there had to be. It's this question that planted the seed for the book you are reading now.

You'll soon discover that the answer doesn't have as much to do with tearing down walls, finding contractors, or managing rehabs as you think.

As I've met and networked with other successful women investors over the years, I've kept this question firmly in the back of my mind. Always looking for that common thread that would lead me to the answer.

This book is the culmination of my conversations with some of the most successful women real estate investors I know about their journey to success. Not celebrity gurus or reality TV stars. Real women, like myself, who are in the trenches, doing it every day. We all achieved success in different ways. Some initially focused on notes and wholesaling, while others focused on fix and flips and rental properties before expanding to other areas of investing. But as you'll see, we all started in the same place in life that you might be right now.

I worked in Corporate America for many years before I started investing in real estate 15 years ago. Not only am I achieving financial freedom, building wealth, and leaving a legacy, but I have more time to spend with family and give back to the community. The tagline for my business, KBN Homes, is *Making neighborhoods great again, one house at a time* and I truly believe in that. Through real estate investing, I'm able to help homeowners in distressed situations as compassionately and fairly as possibly while providing a way for others to purchase through our home ownership program.

Maybe you're also ready to escape corporate America. Maybe the kids are grown and you want to earn extra money. Maybe you've developed an interest from fix-and-flip shows on cable TV.

It doesn't matter whatever got you here; you probably feel a little lost. I know I did in the beginning, not knowing where to start, or where to get help… or knowing the answer to that question.

So, what is the most important thing I need to learn to succeed as a woman real estate investor?

Answer: **You need to learn… about yourself.**

You see, one thing all the women in this book have in common is that we tried to do it all. The most important thing we learned in our journey to success is that we can't do it all and we can't be everything to everyone. We all learned that success is not just about being willing to take on the additional responsibilities as a business owner; it's also about recognizing that there are things in life that we have to be willing to let go of.

As caregivers and homemakers trying to balance work and home lives, we learned the importance of being organized and having a solid support system in place. We developed the discipline to educate ourselves through attending Real Estate Investing meetings, seminars, reading books, watching videos, and listening to podcasts.

You don't have to be the smartest or richest person. You just need common sense and be willing to work hard. Yes, it's true, contrary to the popular reality shows, real estate investing is hard work. It will challenge you in ways that you never thought you could be challenged. But you can make it a lot easier for yourself by finding the right networking group, educational materials, and mentor.

While there are a lot of great books out their covering strategic and tactical methods for winning in real estate investing, I never found one written specifically for women, letting them know they are not alone in this business.

So, it turns out, this isn't just the book I wanted to write... it's the book I needed to write. It's the book I wish I could have read when I was starting out.

I'm so grateful to the women who were willing to share their journey for this book. I learned so much from each of them through our conversations and I'm sure you'll find the knowledge they share will be some of the most valuable of your real estate investing career.

They are true mentors and educators.

I'm always learning and my hope is that this book not only inspires you to take the time to educate yourself about how to be a true, successful real estate investor but also gives you the courage to follow your heart if it's something that you really want to do. You are not alone, you are part of a sisterhood that pulls together and supports one another.

I hope you truly enjoy this book. It was written with you in mind, so thanks so much and good luck on your real estate investing journey!

NANCY WALLACE-LAABS

NANCY WALLACE-LAABS

Nancy Wallace-Laabs is a licensed real estate broker in the state of Texas. She has more than 15 years of real estate investing experience, owns several rental properties, and manages properties in the North DFW area.

Nancy and her husband, Brian Laabs, own KBN Homes, LLC, a real estate investment company that is making neighborhoods great again, one home at a time.

By actively seeking homes that are difficult to sell, and compassionately representing owners in distress, KBN Homes offers hope, relief, and options to sellers while also creating opportunities for investors.

Beginning the Journey

For years, I worked in sales and marketing at United Blood Services, the second largest blood bank in the United States, headquartered in Scottsdale, AZ. I started with the company as a community relations representative. Through hard work, excellent customer service, and marketing expertise, I worked through the ranks to Director of Recruitment.

I traveled extensively throughout the United States, Canada, and England to consult with other blood banks on donor recruitment. I was published in *Transfusion Medicine* regarding a first-time blood donor study I coordinated after 9-11.

In 2005, my husband and I took advantage of the real estate boom in Phoenix, sold our home, and took a leap of faith and moved to Frisco, Texas.

Utilizing the team building, organizational, and time management skills I acquired at United Blood Services, my husband and I founded KBN Homes.

Since then, we have acquired rental homes which we either did the rehab ourselves or oversaw the work being done. We continue to grow our real estate business by incorporating wholesaling, flipping, and buying single-family homes in appreciating areas.

How Real Estate Investing Changed My Life

Investing has given me the ability to branch out into other fields of real estate. I've learned over the years that it's not just about buying houses at 70 percent of ARV. A real estate investment business includes flipping, owner financing, and rental portfolios. I am so grateful for all the opportunities that I have been presented with on my journey as a real estate investor.

Much of real estate investing is networking, mentoring, and continually learning. Each real estate deal I work on allows me to meet people, network, learn from others, and to take all that knowledge and build a successful real estate business.

On Being a Woman Investor

Often, women get into real estate investing as a second career. Maybe the children have all grown, or we're just looking for something different to do, or perhaps we've watched one too many HGTV shows and think it's something that we can do. Of course, if you are in real estate investing, you know the HGTV shows do not tell the entire story.

I have been in management more years than I can count and have always held positions in companies where I was one of the very few female managers. So, when I began investing in real estate, I didn't see any differences. You have to work hard, prove yourself, do your due diligence and more importantly, you must be true to your word. When you're true to your word, people respect you, and they can take to the bank what you're saying to be valid.

Many more skills go into play in investing than just finding real estate deals. You need to be organized and incorporate time management into your day-to-day activities. You must always be consistent.

You need great people skills and should be able to manage people to ensure work is done and done correctly. Whether it's overseeing the renovations of a flip, negotiating prices with a seller, or negotiating vendor prices, those functions all translate from any field, regardless if it's investing in real estate or running a successful company.

So, the journey for women entering into real estate investment might be a little bit different, but we can be equally successful as men in this industry.

On Work-Life Balance

The biggest bonus of real estate investing is that I was able to successfully blend my home life with my real estate investing career. When I say blend, I mean that I'm able to spend more time with my husband and daughter looking for deals. We've gone out together as a family and talked to sellers, have flipped houses, and explored many different opportunities that have presented themselves. We've also been able to take trips together that were focused on real estate investing.

Real estate investing has enhanced my relationship with both my daughter and my husband. I love spending time with them looking at properties and talking with sellers. It's been great to see my daughter learn about real estate investing and take what she's learned since she was about 12 years old and start building her financial freedom. She's very excited about a career in real estate investing.

Also, I firmly believe I'm not a housekeeper, and I do have someone that cleans my house. That frees up my time to work on my business or spend time with my family. Sometimes it's hard for women to let go of some of the smaller things in life, but that's been really important to me to be able to free up my time for either my family or my business.

Being able to manage my home life with my real estate investing career has just been a blessing as it has allowed me to spend more quality time with my family.

Lessons Learned/
What I Wish I Knew

There are many things, but what really sticks out in my mind is I wish I would have known that there were more ways to buy real estate assets than only going to the traditional lenders. Early in my real estate investing career, I spent many days talking to lenders about buying real estate.

There's an old saying that if you find the deal, the money will come. That is true, but where the money will come from depends on your exit strategy. If you need to buy a property fast, there's always hard money lenders and private money lenders, but if you want to hold the property for a long period of time, then you need to work with a lender who understands asset-based lending.

When you buy your first one or two properties, you can probably go through the traditional lenders. My experience has been that the top four lenders are not very investor-friendly.

I also wish I would have known early on the types of relationships I needed to cultivate for buying real estate. One of the first properties I purchased after I reached my max limit on traditional funding was through a loan I secured because of my relationship with another investor who introduced me to a community bank president.

So, there are a lot of lending opportunities out there, but you do have to get out and meet people. In addition to being credit-worthy (and it doesn't mean you must have good credit, it just means that you must have credit), you also have to build your relationships and build your reputation as someone who finds solid deals.

Words of Wisdom

When you're new to real estate investing, focus on why you want to get into this business. It can be a tough business.

It may seem like it would be super easy to make a lot of money in real estate. There's plenty of TV shows following people who are making a lot of money. But it takes time. If you have a day job, don't quit the day job right away. Attend real estate networking meetings, take time to drive around neighborhoods that you might be interested in investing in, and focus on one type of investment strategy, whether that's a buy-and-hold strategy or a fix-and-flip strategy.

Spend some time learning your market. In the Dallas area, it's very competitive, and we have a lot of investors here. A new investor just starting might feel compelled to pay more for a property because they're competing with a lot of different investors on buying property. I see a lot of new investors get excited about their first deal but they didn't really take the time to do their due diligence and so they didn't see that maybe this isn't such a great deal.

Focus on learning about the business. I'm not saying learn everything about all of the different strategies. Attend real estate meetings and start educating yourself. There are several great real estate investing podcasts, and a lot of free information about real estate investing is available online. You don't need to pay tens of thousands of dollars to learn about real estate investing.

In this business, you can start very slow, or you can go as fast as you want. Set your expectations. Be kind to yourself, have patience, and give yourself permission to take a little bit of time to analyze deals. It's a learning process. I've been doing this for a long time, and I'm still learning every day.

Get out there and network and talk to different people. Let others know that you are interested in real estate investing. You'll find a lot of people that are willing to sit down and talk with you. I love going to coffee with people just to tell my story, and I love helping new investors try to figure out where they should start with investing.

If I Could Give Advice to My Newbie Investor Self

Now that I've been doing it for a few years, if I could talk to my new investor self, I would tell her never give up. Don't let your dreams flit away. Keep true to yourself.

Make sure that you have a good support system. If you don't have a good support system at home, then go to networking events or get involved in real estate investing groups in your area.

Don't give up. The deals will come. Be consistent. Don't do something only once, keep going until you master it. And once you've mastered one area of real estate investing, then move to the next.

Remember, you cannot be all things to all people. You won't be able to solve every seller's issue, and won't be 100 percent successful in every single flip. You will make mistakes. That's okay. Allow yourself to make those mistakes and learn them.

In no time, your real estate investing career will be taking off, and you'll be so glad that you did not give up because you can make your dreams come true. You can spend more time with your family, and you can have financial freedom.

Contact Nancy Wallace-Laabs

Business
KBN Homes, LLC

Email
nancy@kbnhomes.com

Phone
469-430-9885

Website
KBNHomes.com

LinkedIn
LinkedIn.com/in/Nancy-Wallace-Laabs

Facebook
Facebook.com/KBNHomesLLC

Twitter
Twitter.com/KBNHomesLLC

YouTube
KBNHomes.com/YouTube

Instagram
Instagram.com/KBNHomesLLC

KRISTIN GERST

KRISTIN GERST

Kristin Gerst has been a full-time real estate investor for 13 years. She has invested in hundreds of both single-family and multi-family properties. Since 2008, Kristin has become an expert in owner finance notes. She has originated several hundred notes and has been training and mentoring other investors in owner financing.

Kristin started Capricorn Mortgage Investments in 2015 and has bought and sold millions of dollars in notes in just the last couple of years.

Kristin is the owner and creator of the successful online company OwnerFinanceDirect.com. She has a BA and MA from the University of North Texas and is bilingual in French and English.

Beginning the Journey

After college, I was a high school teacher. When I got pregnant with my first baby, I thought there was no way I was going to be able to take my baby to daycare. Three months after I had the baby, I was going out of my mind, and my husband noticed. So, he started bringing me real estate investment books. He would go to the bookstore every time he saw I was finished with a book and buy me a new book. After reading four or five books, I said, "You know, I think I can do this. Our next-door neighbor is a realtor, let me call him."

It just so happened that our neighbor specialized in working with investors. He's since long-retired, but he was a bright guy and asked me, "Okay, what do you want to buy?" I told him I had been reading a book on duplexes, tris, and quads and asked him to find me a fourplex. He ended up turning me onto an eight-unit apartment building.

How Real Estate Investing Changed My Life

The thing that's made me most successful in real estate is figuring out clients. I ended up with 61 doors between January 2005 and July 2008 by stumbling into the world of something called "refi cash outs." They don't exist like this anymore, but this was during the boom in 2006-2007.

I was buying properties in East or South Dallas at twenty-five or thirty cents on the dollar down. On day one, I'd buy it and close on it. Then, I would completely rehab it with new electrical, plumbing, etc. On day 12, I would have an appraiser go through the property. On day 14, I would sign a lease, and on the same day, I would refinance at 70 percent of appraisal value.

I would buy a $90,000 home for $40,000 and put about $15,000 into it. Then I would get a loan for $60,000-$63,000, but only be into the property for $45,000. So, I would use the excess to pay off other properties or buy more. I purchased dozens of properties doing that.

On Being a Woman Investor

I see being a woman as an advantage in investing. Nobody expects me to know what I'm talking about until I start talking numbers, mortgages, and the finance behind the flip. I can tell you in less than five minutes if it will be a good flip just by hearing the numbers.

I like to work with brand-new women investors because sometimes they don't know how to get started. They may be recently divorced, or the kids are grown and moved out, or they want to make extra money. A lot of women will say, "I don't have any money." My role is to help those women learn from others who have had success, where they got started, and what they think the pitfalls are.

I also promote women in real estate investing. I sit on an all-women lunch council, and the majority of the groups that I promote have been women. We're all driven and entrepreneurial.

Everybody you talk to, man or woman, has something that they could teach you. Don't pretend you know it all and don't be cold and completely businesslike, or nobody will want to do business with you.

You have to give respect to get respect. Especially with contractors because they are disrespected a lot of times, mostly by men. Some men don't feel that they have to show decency to their contractors.

I have a great relationship with all my contractors because I'm down to Earth. I am polite and pleasant and fun. My contractors have been working for me for 12 years, so I already know that they respect me enough to keep working for me. They give me great deals, and they always answer my phone calls.

I have also done work with women-only contracting companies. I have great relationships with those contractors as well.

On Work Life Balance

At first, I managed my work-life balance very poorly. I started investing when I was pregnant with my youngest, and I had a one-year-old. My boys are now 13 and 14. They have always seen me working, and they would often come to job sites with me. One would be in a little snuggly baby carrier, and the other one would just run around. After we finished at the job site, we would go to the Arboretum and play. So, I balanced it like that when they were young. Once they started school, it was easier.

Now, I'm basically a chauffeur for my boys. I take them to school and pick them up after school and get them to any activities they might have.

I tell women to delegate as much as they can. You can break repetitive tasks down into five steps or less and farm them out. You don't need to clean your house. I know you think you do, but the hours you spend doing that could instead be spent hunting down leads.

We have a housekeeper two days a week, a laundry service, and a yard service. I am shocked when I meet women with one or two tiny babies and somehow their house always seems clean. I'm sure it wasn't unless they were expecting people to show up, but it just always seemed wonderful.

I can do most of my work from anywhere in the world. I deal primarily with investment banks because that's who my buyers are. So, I make sure that my investment banks are happy.

I've got one rehab going on right now, and so I keep up with that and pop in to check that it's going well. But do I spend all my time there? No. I get photos all the time, and my project manager tells me what's going on. I trust him.

I have four virtual assistants that are all women. I love to employ women in third-world countries especially those that are under Islamic rule. These women can't leave their house on a regular basis to go to work, and might not be able to get a job period. My assistants have been working for me for six or seven years, and they are all wonderful.

Lessons Learned/ What I Wish I Knew

If you've got debt that you're servicing, it completely takes away from everything else that's going on. So, if you want to do long-term cash flow, if you buy four properties, you keep one. You cannot keep the whole world.

April 2009 was one of the worst times in my real estate investing career. Everything had already gone to hell. The outdoor air conditioner units were stolen from five of my properties. Suddenly, I had to pay out tens of thousands of dollars. I was just beginning to owner finance everything, but I hadn't totally gotten there yet. I wish I had less debt to pay on at the time.

Words of Wisdom

Start with wholesaling. Team up with a successful wholesaler that can assign you some tasks and show you different ways to find properties. Once you find the properties, partner with them on the deal.

After the crash in 2008, I had 61 doors all rented with section eight vouchers. I had cash flow, but I couldn't buy anything else. I wanted to make money doing something else in real estate. So, I started wholesaling, and I did a couple of wholesale deals on a small level. I reached out to friends that were doing a lot of wholesaling business and asked to work with them. We split the profits 50/50. I was looking at 40-50 foreclosures a week and putting anything under contract that we could get at the right price. It was great to start with somebody who was already successful.

You can learn a lot from the many real estate books that are available. But I do think you need to get out there. You have to take the step; you have to try it. Sign up for a local seminar or class on something you're interested in learning. You can read blog articles and watch YouTube videos. Don't spend $20,000 or $30,000 on a seminar or program until you've tried using free or low-cost resources first.

If I Could Give Advice to My Newbie Investor Self

First, delegate responsibility. I wish I hadn't waited seven years to do this.

Second, get rid of all underlying debt. In real estate, you have to borrow money, but make it revolving debt so that if you have a million-dollar line you're buying properties with, make sure you pay back some of that debt.

Avoid long-term debt. It's good to have a little debt, but once we have another dip in the market, if you have a lot of long-term debt, it's a liability. They are not assets because if you stop performing in any one of those, it snowballs.

Contact Kristin Gerst

Business
Capricorn Mortgage Investments

Website
CapricornMortgage.com

Email
Info@capricornmortgage.com

LinkedIn
Linkedin.com/in/Kristin-Gerst-a2a6a66/

AMY SAYRE

AMY SAYRE

Recognizing a need in the investor community for private party lender loan servicing, Amy founded August REI, LLC in June of 2009. Beginning with just 25 loans, Amy has grown the August REI portfolio to $313,000,000+ with an enviable default rate of 1.80%. Amy's background in mortgage loan servicing, property management, and management of a residential appraisal firm have served her well.

Amy remains as the President and CEO of August REI and directs the compliance required by state and federal regulation. Amy continues to build the portfolio with the August REI mission statement in mind: *Never compromise trust, timeliness, and quality of service to any client.*

Amy graduated from the University of Texas-Arlington with a B.A. in Interdisciplinary Studies; she lives in Rockwall, Texas with her husband and their three sons.

Beginning the Journey

I started in real estate investing keeping the books for my family's investments and managing the real estate appraisal office. The note servicer we were using billed us per collection call, but they were only leaving voicemail messages and not always collecting the payments. The monthly servicing fees varied which affected my financial predictions and my memorized transactions in QuickBooks.

One Easter, I was decorating deviled eggs in the kitchen and telling, or perhaps complaining to, my mother that the servicer was not doing a good enough job. My mother turned and said, "You have two options – do it yourself or get over it." The gauntlet had been thrown down. I decided I would do it myself.

I started servicing loans for my family, then family friends, and then other investors. I was getting so many calls that I finally had to say I could not accept more clients until my son started school in August – and that's where I came up with the name *August Real Estate Investments*.

The most challenging part of getting started in loan servicing was getting the right software to do the job. At first, I had *NoteSmith* which I refer to as a '72 Volkswagen with a flat tire. The system had a low price point, and we were able to service 100-150 loans on that system.

Then we moved up to *The Mortgage Office* system through Applied Business Software, and the buy-in for two licenses was $36,000. Now we carry 17 licenses. Our biggest expense has been in software.

We gained new business primarily from referrals until 2015 when I started marketing. One main advantage we have is that we report to credit. A lot of people want their borrowers to be able to report to credit, and in doing so, their borrowers can refinance if there is a wrap, which is to their benefit.

How Real Estate Investing Changed My Life

Real estate investing has changed my family's future. It has provided us with financial freedom and has allowed me to meet many wonderful people and make some great relationships.

On Being a Woman Investor

The main thing I've experienced is that when dealing with contractors, because they are primarily men, they sometimes don't want to take orders from females. Once, I had to take my husband with me to a job site to get a contractor to do what I wanted.

It was challenging and irritating because my husband knew nothing of what I was trying to get across. I think the contractor thought I didn't know what I was doing. When I would ask him to do something, it never got done. Then my husband would request the same thing, and it would get done.

Once, we were having a deck with a patio cover built at our house. I wanted to replace a window in the master bedroom with a French door. My husband called and said the contractor told him they couldn't do it because there was an inch difference on the sides. I said an inch is nothing and told him to put the contractor on the phone. I told the contractor, "Move the jack studs out, beef up my header, put the door in, or pack up your crap and leave. I will find someone else who will do the work." And he said, "That's fine. We've got it, ma'am."

My husband doesn't know what jack studs are. I do, but the contractor only listened to me because I told him to pack up and leave. So, when dealing with contractors, you need to have a backup, or you have to be overly assertive.

On Work Life Balance

My husband is at home and takes care of our family. He manages the house, runs errands, and makes dinner. We also have a cleaning lady to help around the house.

Some nights I'm up until 1:00 am finishing up work, so not having to focus on cooking and cleaning helps me focus on my business.

Lessons Learned/ What I Wish I Knew

I wish I had leveraged my capital more on the first one or two deals.

Also, every time I did something new, or there was a unique situation or problem to solve, I should have written down the details and created a flow chart. *If this happens, go here. If you can't get your water turned on, this is where you go. If it's a certain county, always have a water key in the back of your trunk.* I could have created processes more quickly and built systems to automate tasks.

Words of Wisdom

Focus on one method of real estate investing and learn everything about that first, whether it's wholesaling, subject to, or flipping. Find someone to follow around and learn by watching them.

I come from a real estate family, and when I was younger, I didn't want to follow my mom around. I wanted to prove I was an adult and could do it myself. I wish I had taken my mother up on her offer instead of being stubborn because I ended up doing my first deal with my mom anyway, and I learned a lot from her throughout the process.

In the beginning, partnering with someone who knows the business, even if you don't make as much money, is a really good way to go because they have the knowledge and can help you avoid making costly mistakes.

A partner can introduce you to other investors and their contractors, and you'll make great contacts. By working with a reputable investor, you can establish credibility in the industry.

If I Could Give Advice to My Newbie Investor Self

Don't overthink things. (I'm an analyst by trade, so I analyze things to the nth degree.) Put systems in place for handling different situations so you can move more quickly.

If you can find a property and it's a good deal, you'll find a way to make it work. Put it under contract, and then you'll find the money, or you will find the partners to make it happen. If you worry and wait too long, you will miss out on some good deals.

Contact Amy Sayre

Business
August Real Estate Investments, LLC

Website
AugustREI.com

Email
amy@augustrei.com

Phone
469-701-2555

SANDRA J. NESBITT

SANDRA J. NESBITT

Sandra Nesbitt is the founder and owner of Reddtrow Properties, LLC in Allen, TX. Reddtrow is a real estate investment company that buys, sells, and rents residential properties for a profit.

Sandra started Reddtrow after graduating college in the late 1990s while working full-time in the publishing industry in New York City.

After running this business successfully part-time, Sandra quit her job in February 2005 and focused on expanding Reddtrow full-time.

In the Fall of 2007, Sandra moved operations to Dallas at the beginning of the housing crisis. The transition was not easy, but eventually, Sandra established Reddtrow as one of the leading residential real estate investment companies in the Dallas/Fort Worth metroplex.

Beginning the Journey

I am originally from Bronx, NY and I've been investing in real estate for 20 years. After I graduated college in February 1999, I realized that I was going to have to work at a JOB (just over broke) for 40 years to get a pension for retirement. I didn't know exactly what, but I knew I needed to find something else to secure a better financial future.

I couldn't find a job immediately after I graduated and I was living at home in New York. My mother received some junk mail that offered a voucher for a free trip to the Caribbean if I attended a free real estate seminar on Long Island. So, we went, and it was a big sales pitch promoting a $5,000 mentor program. We left without buying the program.

Exactly a week later, one of their salesmen called me, and sold me! I was still not working and figured this was something to do until I found a job. By the way, I had just paid off $12,000 in credit card debt. I was now committed to making this work. I told myself this was the last thing that I would charge and would work just to pay this off.

The program was a 50/50 partnership where an experienced Real Estate "Guru" would teach you to do deals if you brought in the leads. But each time I would give them a lead, they said it wouldn't work.

I found out later that none of their deals worked for other members of the group in the New York City area. It turned out this was a fraud from a group in Florida, so I lost $5,000. I eventually found a job in the publishing industry. I had this debt, and I just wanted to pay it off and frankly didn't care about being successful with real estate investing.

So, for two years, I was all over the place trying to figure this out. I was in New Jersey, upstate Westchester Country, and finally Connecticut trying to make it work, but I was spinning my wheels.

Then, I bought a much cheaper course about vacant houses for a thousand dollars. I followed it step-by-step and finally closed my first deal. Right after that, I got my very first big deal, and the rest is history!

How Real Estate Investing Changed My Life

It's been a character and confidence builder. I've gotten used to rejections, and I'm not afraid to ask for anything now. If they say yes, that's great; if they say no, then I move on. I don't take it personally or let it carry over to my personal life.

It's taught me a lot about real estate, the basics of buying and selling a house, and sales. If I were to sell my own house, I wouldn't need a realtor. I'm very informed about estimating repairs, home values, and marketing.

I get to meet all different types of people from all walks of life. I can find something to identify with and build rapport instantly. That's what I like best about real estate investing.

I've become an expert problem solver and marketer. I've had some challenging deals this year, and we really had to dig deep and be resourceful to find a solution.

Finally, it has provided me with tremendous flexibility and financial freedom. I learned everything from scratch and didn't stop until I was successful.

On Being a Woman Investor

I've never had this experience, but other women in real estate that I talk to have said that often contractors think they can't make decisions or don't know how to estimate repairs. Contractors will ask them: Who do you work for? Who's coming to the estimate repairs or make an offer? (Especially with fire-damaged houses.)

I've been in this business long enough and when they hear me speak, they know I know what I'm talking about and any concerns with age, race, or gender all go away.

Some sellers prefer working with a female investor. They're more comfortable meeting in the evenings or allowing a female in their home at night.

On Work Life Balance

I've worked from home and worked at an office. Each has its pros and cons. When I work from home, I take breaks, make believe I'm stepping into an office, and get dressed like I would if I were going to an office building.

There are certainly distractions. I try not to stay on the road for most of the day. It's very tempting to take a nap, watch TV, etc. The key is to focus and stick to the highest priorities for the day.

I believe in working and playing hard and have been fortunate to travel to amazing places around the world. By the way, I did make it to the Caribbean.

Lessons Learned/ What I Wish I Knew

I wish I would have been laser-focused, consistent, and more disciplined. I should have picked one niche, mastered it, and then moved on to another real estate investment niche.

Words of Wisdom

Get out of your head! Self-doubt, fear, and procrastination will kill your dreams and aspirations. Consistently work on your mindset because you will get discouraged. You're going to experience a lot of disappointment, but you can achieve your goals, whether it's wholesaling, rentals, rehabs, or something else.

It's going to take hard work and time, especially in today's market. Stay focused and always be consistent. I find a lot of new investors try a little bit of this, then try a little bit of that, and they just give up too quickly.

Educate and invest in yourself. If you are on a limited budget, listen to YouTube videos. I like quick 10-15 minute videos. Read books. I just finished reading *Think and Grow Rich* by Napoleon Hill, and I'm about to start *10X Rule* by Grant Cardone. You should be reading at least one book per month, attend seminars, masterminds, and most importantly, take massive action.

You need to build a really good team with other experienced professionals that have your best interests at heart. If you show that you're a doer, you're going to attract people that get things done. If you're just thinking about doing this and that, no one will take you seriously, and they won't want to work with you.

Find a mentor. I've paid tens of thousands, probably six figures, in the last 20 years on mentors, and it's worth every penny. Do your due diligence and don't throw your money at any person.

Be careful if you're just starting and you have little money. Try to find a local mentor that will work with you, and you need to do everything that they say. If you're serious, you will attract a great mentor that might mentor you for free. There's a lot of free information out there, but if you want to really take this to the next level, you're going to have to pay for a mentor.

If I Could Give Advice to My Newbie Investor Self

Whatever you focus on, think about the future. A lot of people are attracted to wholesaling to make a quick buck. I started in wholesaling, and I still wholesale. It's a pretty good job and pays well if you know what you're doing. But what are you doing with that money? Spend some money, but also build wealth. For every two-five wholesale deals you buy, buy another property to hold that will generate passive income and create wealth.

Contact Sandra J. Nesbitt

Email Address
info@reddtrowproperties.com

Phone Number
214-306-9740

Business Name
Reddtrow Properties, LLC

Website
ReddtrowProperties.com

Facebook
Facebook.com/Reddtrow

LinkedIn
LinkedIn.com/company/Reddtrow-Properties-LLC

Twitter
Twitter.com/Reddtrow

YouTube
YouTube.com/channel/UCx2dNvq2MLBP_auuuj7T5nw

JAMIE BURLESON WOOLEY

JAMIE BURLESON WOOLEY

Jamie Burleson Wooley began investing in Real Estate in early 2016. Her company, W Streets, Inc., based in Dallas, Texas, did over 200 deals in 2017 and 2018. About 75 percent of her business is wholesaling, and the other 25 percent is rehabbing properties and flipping or holding as rentals.

Beginning the Journey

From an early age, I always thought outside of the box. I was never into doing the social norm such as going to school and knowing what I wanted to be when I grew up. I never felt that I fit into that mold, but that was the only mold I really knew. So, I went off to college for a couple of years, and I realized it wasn't for me.

I started a family young, which I was not prepared to do. I became a mother and a wife a lot sooner than I had anticipated, but it was a blessing and a surprise. I stayed at home with my daughter for the first five years because that was very important for me.

During that time, I sold clothing online because the entrepreneur vibe was always running through my veins, and I thought maybe that's something I would enjoy doing. I purchased clothes from California and resold them here in Dallas. I liked it, but I wasn't passionate about it. It was just a ticket to a paycheck at the end of the week, so that was short-lived.

Then, I started a golf marketing company. I played golf competitively in high school and college, so golf was something at which I excelled. I went to several golf courses and convinced them to agree to offer either discounted or free rounds of golf. I put all the offers from about ten different high-level golf courses in Dallas and Fort Worth on one card, and I sold those online. I made money doing this, but it wasn't something I was passionate about, nor did I see it evolving into something that I could retire from in the future.

My Dad owns a company, and he suggested that I come to work for him until I could figure out what I wanted to do next. I started out doing basic administrative tasks: answering phones and doing some dispatch stuff. Soon after, the office manager left and being a daddy's girl, I decided this was maybe something that I could take on and do a good job for him, and learn a little bit. So that's what I did.

At the time, I didn't consider that this would be something I would do long term, but I ended up staying in that position for eight years, and I learned so much during that time. I sat in on lots of meetings, and I learned how to structure projects, how to organize, how to hire people, how to let people go, and how to manage people all without knowing that's what I was doing.

One day, I just looked around and said this can't be all there is for me. This is not what I wanted. Like a lot of people, I watched HGTV. I just loved watching people renovate houses. When my husband and I bought our first house, we were young, so that also meant we were broke. We renovated the house ourselves, and I loved doing that. At the time, I didn't think of it as a business; I just focused on taking this old house and making it look good for us to move in.

But I thought, *You know what? I loved every second of doing that.* I immediately decided that's what I was going to do and got my real estate license, not knowing if I needed it or not for investing. In the evenings, while my husband and daughter were sleeping, I was studying and learning.

No one even knew that I was doing it until the day I got my license and I told my family, "This is what I am going to do." I gave my dad four months' notice and said I would hire and train my replacement. That's how I started my journey into real estate.

How Real Estate Investing Changed My Life

Real estate investing has changed my life on so many different levels. It's changed me personally. I am more confident and have the mindset to do what others say is unattainable or cannot be accomplished within a set time.

Real estate has changed my family also. I think my husband is a bit relieved knowing that I'm bringing in a good amount of income. He's no longer the primary person responsible for our family's financial now and financial future.

It has allowed me to meet some of the most amazing, giving, friendly, and loving people ever.

It has allowed me to discover systems and learn processes, how to manage people, all the ins and outs that come with running a business, and how to build a legacy and help others.

I only had a mere glimpse of these things before I got deep into real estate. The things that I've learned have just been amazing, and I've been able to accomplish a lot of things that most people didn't think could be accomplished, especially by a female in this industry. I don't know any other female owner that's running a company and doing over 100 deals per year.

And so, real estate investing has shown me that whatever you want to do is possible if you set your mind to do it, take action, and have the appropriate people in place.

On Being a Woman Investor

Mindset is important. I never set out with the mindset that there would be any differences for me as a woman real estate investor. I always looked at it as you're going to get back what you put into it. Growing up, I played golf which is a male-dominated sport. Ninety percent of the people at the golf course are men. So, I have always understood that if you excel at something that is male-dominated, you will get respect.

I knew that to make it in this industry words were not going to be what would get me the respect or get me in the door or get the conversation with the right people. I needed to take action and show results. So, I knew going into this, I needed to be results-oriented to attract the people that would be necessary to succeed going forward, and that's what I set out to do, and that's what I achieved.

On Work-Life Balance

Balancing being a mother, a wife, and a business owner while also running my daughter to club volleyball practice, church, and tutoring is something that I deal with every day. It is not easy. My husband is also an entrepreneur, so he is very busy with his own business, which has nothing to do with my industry or my business.

Although I also work, I've always been the one to take my daughter to school, pick her up, make sure she gets her homework done. I take her to meetings, make sure that all her activities are scheduled on the calendar and that we make it to each event, and that she gets whatever she needs for the craft that's due on Friday at school.

So, it is a lot, and I have managed to deal with that. My husband and I have had to come together as a couple and as a team and say, look, I understand you're busy, but here are some things that we're going to have to change up a little bit so I can have some help. And that has been a push and pull for the past couple of years, and we've found a way to make it work.

But it is not easy because as mothers, as women, we are more nurturing, and our kiddos need to be nurtured and loved. Although they definitely can get that from their father, that's something in which the mom plays a huge role. So, there are sometimes that the business has to take a backseat or I have to go to a speaking event or go out of town when I would rather be at home with my family. It's a sacrifice, but I'm willing to make those sacrifices for what I see in the future, the legacy that I'm building.

I'm probably not going to answer my phone at 9:00 at night if I'm watching my daughter's volleyball game or if I'm saying prayers with her at night.

There are certain times that I will not be available because I'm a mom and I'm okay with that. Everyone that is a part of my team knows that, and it's understood with my employees. You just have to manage it a little bit differently. Many men that have the very same role that I have, but in our household, I've had to take it day by day and make it work.

Lessons Learned/
What I Wish I Knew

I have to be honest and say that luckily my mentors were very good and prepared me for a lot of what went on during this time of my life. But I would have liked to have known that there are going to be times when you may want to crawl into a fetal position and you think that nothing is going to work out or get better. But if you keep pushing, you can work through that.

There have been days over the years that I was frustrated with managing people, or the bank account was getting low, or a house remodel took six weeks longer, or a contractor took money from me. So, I think that the struggles are not talked about as often as they should be.

If you're a business owner, you're going to struggle. I would have liked to have known that most other business owners have had the feelings that I had and experienced the moments that I had. I try to share struggles throughout the journey because I think some people do get in certain situations and think, wow, I wonder if that person ever had to go through this. They probably did go through it, but they might not have been as vocal about it.

Words of Wisdom

First, focus on what you want to do. There are so many different things to do in real estate investing. You can wholesale, buy and hold rental properties, or fix and flip. You can have single-family, multi-family, land, or notes. There are several options available within each of these niches, and it can become very overwhelming and what we call *Shiny Object Syndrome*. So, when you decide that this is going to be a path that you want to take now or ten years from now, you need to pick one niche and get really good at that.

Second, you need to find a mentor. It can be someone that will mentor you for free, someone that you pay, or a group. It doesn't matter what type of mentor it as long as they have the time and resources to help you. It's very important to find someone or something that you are going to follow that has step-by-step action plans to get you to where you need to be.

It's important to know that you cannot expect everything to change quickly or for money to be coming in quickly if you are not taking quick action. Expect for there to be failures along the way. Learn and grow from those failures, and know that everyone else has gone through those same things and that it will all be okay in the end.

Finally, expect to make certain sacrifices in order to get to the next level you want to be, to be able to provide for your family what you were hoping to provide.

If I Could Give Advice to My Newbie Investor Self

I would tell her to never give up, to always have a plan, to have a group or a network of people to support you through this journey, and that no thought or dream is ever too big if you're willing to put in the work.

Contact Jamie Burleson Wooley

Business
W Streets, LLC

Email
jamie@thewholesalingchick.com

Phone
972-468-1089

Facebook
Facebook.com/Jamie.Wooley.1

Instagram
Instagram.com/MsJamieWooley

LinkedIn
LinkedIn.com/in/Jamie-Wooley-b9b936109

LOLITA SHERIOW

LOLITA SHERIOW

Lolita Sheriow, aka "Take Action Lo."

After surviving personal tragedy, Lo found peace and purpose in business through helping others become successful in business and life.

Lo and her business partner have a full-service real estate investment company that assists homeowners, buyers and investors with all their real estate needs.

Her coaching program, "Take Action Real Estate Wholesaling" teaches others how to get started in real estate investing.

Lo also has a digital marketing company that focuses on branding and lead generation for realtors and real estate professionals using Facebook Advertising and Video Marketing.

Lo provides free content and resources that have helped thousands of people with her popular "Take Action Real Estate Investing" podcast and "Take Action with Lo" YouTube channel that focuses on real estate investing and marketing tips.

Lo served in the United States Army Reserves, was a professional singer, and appeared on Showtime's *At the Apollo with Steve Harvey*. She has a passion for helping young people and supports the Boys and Girls Club of America.

She enjoys spending time with family, traveling, dancing, singing and teaching others!

Her life's motto is... Live, Love, Learn and Laugh!

Beginning the Journey

I've always been entrepreneurial. My first business was a lawn care service in the summer after my junior year of high school. In 2004, I started working for Countrywide Home Loans and was there until 2007.

During that time, the housing market and the economy were terrible. In 2006, a mentor advised me to look at real estate investing. So, I did a lot of research and networking at some of the local REI groups in the Dallas/Fort Worth area specifically to learn how to wholesale. I was still working full time for Countrywide, but when I was laid off in 2007, I just jumped with both feet in and haven't looked back.

How Real Estate Investing Changed My Life

It has given me the ability to make a lot of money, but more importantly, it's allowed me to be able to spend some of the most priceless time with my family. I'm huge on family. Family is a big part of my life. I became an investor for financial freedom and the flexibility to be able to do what I want to do.

I was recently able to take a trip with my mom, my uncle, and my partner to celebrate my uncle's 50th birthday in Hawaii. All of the times that I have been able to spend with them and take trips have been priceless. So, it has definitely changed my life.

On Being a Woman Investor

When I first started, there were more men than women in real estate investing. There were times where information was shared maybe with some of my counterparts that wasn't freely shared with me. But I never let that stop me. I just moved on to someone else and didn't take it personally. It didn't make me want to give up. If anything, it motivated me.

I've learned how to stand my ground, and a lot of that comes with experience and confidence. Just continue to network with other investors that you click with. You can build those lasting relationships with other investors, whether it's men or women.

On Work-Life Balance

It's an ongoing battle, but I can say over the last ten years, I've gotten better. You have to create a schedule and have a routine. Separate work-related tasks from things that are family-oriented. For example, I schedule time on my calendar every Saturday to cut off from work to be with my family, and that's what I do.

There are conflicts sometimes such as a big event, or I'm speaking somewhere, or my business partner has an engagement, but those are exceptions. Is it always going to be perfect? Of course not. You're going to have things that pop up, but maintaining a calendar and having a routine will help you balance your business and family life.

Lessons Learned/ What I Wish I Knew

I wish I would have gotten a mentor sooner when I first started investing in real estate. And I wish I would have asked more questions. I come from a do-it-yourself family. Your mindset has to be different when you're an entrepreneur who wants to grow and scale a business. You can't do it all yourself, and you have to learn how to ask for help and how to outsource.

I also wish I had known more about partnerships and joint ventures. Partnerships can be great, and partnerships can be a nightmare. Do your research when you're looking to do a joint venture or do business with people. Search for them online, investigate them, and ask other well-known active investors in that area if they know them or if they've done business with that person. Also, ask for the testimonials from other investors and clients that they've worked with. Get a history their work ethic and what other people have said about them and what's out there.

Early in my career, I got involved with real estate investing and partnered with an investor that was buying subject-to deals that we found in his particular market. We had a partnership where I would find the deals, and he would pay me. It was mainly wholesaling with subject-to deals. So, we did a few deals, and things were going well. He was very resourceful and helpful.

Long story short, after a couple of years, I got a phone call from a seller of a subject-to deal that my partner had purchased from us. My partner stopped making the mortgage payments, and she was about to lose the house to foreclosure. My partner wasn't answering his phone, so she started calling me.

She was furious, and she had every right to be. But I explained to her, again, about the contract she signed. She complained on the Internet, and it was terrible because that was one of the things I always feared going into businesses: having a negative review or a deal going south for whatever reason.

That was a hard lesson learned. I should've done more research to learn more about this particular investor because it turned out was that he had not only done that to our client, but he had done this with other people that he had partnered with as well. So that's why I say do your research.

I've also had several great partnerships. There's an investor that has bought a lot of deals from us, wholesale, subject-to, whatever, over the last four or five years with no issues.

Words of Wisdom

Find a really good mentor and join a Real Estate Investment (REI) group or mastermind that can add value and provide the resources to help you.

At first, try to find someone local that you can work with and connect with as a mentor or a coach. You want to find somebody that's been there for a while and has had success because then they will have relationships and resources that you can utilize. That can save you a lot of time and frustration.

If you sign up with a guru that's out of state, then you're just having conversations on the phone. I've worked with other clients that came from that environment, and each one said it was a nightmare and they wasted their money. So, find a local group or mastermind that you can also tie in and connect with and go for it.

Expect to learn some of the critical strategies in real estate investing, whether it's wholesaling, or buy-and-hold, etc. Get the right information to be able to take action, to get results, to get deals, to get housing and set realistic goals. A realistic goal for someone new is to be able to close one or two deals within 30 to 60 days. That's absolutely attainable.

If I Could Give Advice to My Newbie Investor Self

Focus on one strategy, master that first, and connect with a local expert that has mastered it and find a way to work with them. With real estate investing, there are so many ways that you can make money: as a wholesaler; you can buy, fix and flip; you can buy and hold; you can buy notes; you can do subject-to deals. I see a lot of new investors get overwhelmed trying to learn multiple strategies at one time. So, just master one to start.

For a free audio of Lolita's

7 Secrets to Real Estate Wholesaling the Gurus Don't Share

visit TakeActionLo.com

Contact Lolita Sheriow

Email

lnsheriow@gmail.com

Phone

(972) 827-8947

Business

Harrtstone Management Inc.

Website

Harrtstone.com

Facebook

Facebook.com/LoSheriow

LinkedIn

LinkedIn.com/in/LolitaSheriow

Twitter

Twitter.com/LoSheriow

YouTube

YouTube.com/LoSheriow

Podcast

Podcast.takeactionlo.com

SUE ABRAMS

SUE ABRAMS

Sue Abrams-Rainger's infatuation with real estate began when her mom launched a second career as a Realtor, in Kansas City. Sue launched her own real estate business in 2015. Today, she is buying and selling houses using various strategies for long-term passive income and more immediate profit as well.

Prior to real estate investment, Sue owned a successful corporate video production company and was a TV news anchor and reporter in several US cities. Sue was born in New York City and raised in Westport, CT and Overland Park, KS. She has lived more than 20 years in North Texas and considers herself an Almost-Native Texan.

Beginning the Journey

My husband and I have always been interested in real estate. In 1999, I started a video production company that was very successful. I was in a bad accident and wasn't able to pursue that field as aggressively as I had been doing.

The technology was always changing, and it just wasn't as lucrative as it had been. So, I decided to make a career change. I attended some real estate investing classes that gave me more information to go forth and conquer.

How Real Estate Investing Changed My Life

I love that I'm so busy all the time. I like to be a productive person, and this allows me to do so. It's a good income, but it's never guaranteed. There are a couple of risks. I'm very risk averse so that part is a downside that I just have to live with because I really enjoy the rest of it.

On Being a Woman Investor

Most of my work is in wholesaling, so I don't see a difference because I'm dealing with the end consumer, which is the seller. But on fix and flips that I've done or owner-finance renovations where I have to deal with contractors, I definitely see that contractors treat women a little differently than male counterparts.

I would say that what I've experienced is the same in other fields; if you're an opinionated woman who is vocal, you're seen as a bitch or a hysterical woman. A vocal guy would just be an authoritative guy who knows what he's doing.

On Work-Life Balance

I struggle with work-life balance and would say that's the one aspect of real estate that I really don't like. There's a lot that goes on, and some days I feel as if I work 10, 12, or 14 hours. I do enlist the help of my husband at times. He has a full-time job with insurance benefits, and he needs to be fresh as a daisy for that.

I haven't had that time to find someone who's trustworthy that can help me out part-time, but I'm looking to do that soon. We're in a temporary location right waiting to move into the house that we're renovating. But I would recommend for anyone else, if you're really busy, make sure you have a helping hand, so it doesn't consume your life.

Lessons Learned/ What I Wish I Knew

One of my first deals was a wholesale deal, and that went okay. It was challenging, but I learned a lot from it. The other two were subject-to deals, and I wish that I had done more due diligence. I will say when you're screening people for owner finance, go with your gut, but also do your due diligence.

I wish my partner and I had done a credit check and a criminal background check on one of the people that we owner-financed to because it really turned out to be quite disastrous. He had been in bankruptcy several times before. He had a long list of creditors. He'd been incarcerated. Little did we know, he was also a pathological liar.

This situation just turned out to be a nightmare. It's been a year of no payments. We've had a couple of lawyers to help us fight all his bankruptcies and, hopefully, things are going forward with this third attempt at foreclosing on him, but he's very wily, and he's very adept at navigating the system.

Even with that problem, I still love real estate. I don't win every deal, but I've way more than compensated for that loss by all the other winning deals. So, in the end, it's just of one of those where I wish I knew was how to screen someone very thoroughly before allowing them to buy an owner-finance house.

Words of Wisdom

Everyone's different and so what might work for one woman might not work for another one. If you haven't previously had a career in a male-dominated field, be aware that you may encounter some differences in the way that you're treated, but that's okay because you can deal with it if you recognize it.

If someone's not respectful to you and doesn't acknowledge your valid concerns that you have presented professionally, then you're not going to work with that person again.

If I Could Give Advice to My Newbie Investor Self

Ignore all the clichés – jump in with both feet, fake it till you make it, blah, blah, blah. Take it slow and be prudent. You don't have to do your first six deals in the first six months of real estate investing.

Make sure you have a good mix of real estate activities that balance out risks versus rewards. Don't put too much pressure on yourself and don't let yourself be consumed with competitive thoughts.

When you see other people that are doing a bunch of deals, know that you'll be there too. So just give it time, keep working, be persistent. Keep at it, notice what's not working, and tweak things going forward. Eventually, you will get there. Just keep at it.

Contact Sue Abrams

Business Name
UTRP, LLC

Email
sue@rangertxsolutions.com

Website
RangerTxSolutions.com

Phone
(469) 843-3498

SUSAN TIERNEY

SUSAN TIERNEY

Before becoming a Real Estate investor in January of 2016, Susan spent 30 years in Marketing and Public Relations, engaging consumers on a local, regional and national level. Her experience leveraging all forms of media, such as television, radio, print, digital, social, direct mail, etc., for establishing a brand, creating awareness, and sparking consumers to take action is quite extensive.

She also has a proven track record of helping companies bring their products to the masses via big box retailers such as Target, Walmart, and Best Buy. After 30 years in the business, Susan was ready for a change and pursued a career as a real estate investor.

In August of 2016, Susan partnered with Scott Horne and formed S2Equities which specializes in helping people through the foreclosure process by offering sound, practical advice and solutions. In their first two years, they purchased, rehabbed, and owner financed over 60 properties.

They also formed a Hispanic lending company called CasaBella Tejas, specializing in working with the Hispanic community creating homeownership opportunities.

Beginning the Journey

I was in sales and marketing for 30 years. I did public relations and national media sales, and I was bored stiff. I worked from home, and I had a lot of clients. I wanted to find something that I could wake up excited about and jump out of bed to get started right away. I could do my job at the time in my sleep. I thought if I had to write one more press release or had to meet with one more editor, I was going to scream.

It was the end of the year, and I decided I was going to find a new career. I always loved watching HGTV shows. I knew I could do that, and I'd always say I that would do it when I retire. Then, I received an ad in the mail for a traveling show with Christina and Tarek. I grabbed a realtor friend of mine, and she came with me. We signed up and paid about $99 for a weekend class. After that weekend, I knew I wanted to do this for the rest of my life.

After doing some research, I signed up with a nationwide real estate investment coaching program. Then I convinced three of my girlfriends that were looking for a career change to join me and that's how we started HomeGirls. I immersed myself in the coaching program and learned everything I could and just got out there.

My first deal was wholesaling my mother's house in Rockwall. It had been hit by a tornado, and only the frame was left. Vultures were knocking on our door and offering her $5,000 to $10,000. I sold what was left of the house for $40,000 and made my mom all that money.

Then I focused on training and attending REI group meetings. Aside from my mother's house, I didn't have a deal for six months. I kept getting leads. I knew how to market it because I'd been doing that for 30 years, but I couldn't get a deal. I kept going to different people at the clubs and say, "Hey, I got this deal, you want to go in and with me?" But we could never close the deal. And, then I met Scott Horne and brought him a deal, and closed it right away.

I brought them another deal and closed quickly. All the deals were foreclosures with strange liens or probate issues that Scott could get through when other people couldn't. After we worked together on a few deals, I suggested we should form a company. Scott was ending a 25-year partnership, and the timing just worked.

That was two years ago, and we just purchased our 68th property. I do all the marketing and find the properties, and then I handle all the rehabs. We do owner financing, so it works.

I'm fortunate I have a husband who has a good job, but with owner financing, we pay down that debt. We don't take that interest spread, and we apply the down payment to the principal. So, I keep saying in seven or eight years I'm going to be really, really wealthy. But right now, I need a paycheck, so we will flip. We will sell a few houses retail, but I prefer owner financing.

How Real Estate Investing Changed My Life

It changed my life to have something I was passionate and excited about again. It's really marketing to me now. My partner will say it's all about financing. He's the numbers guy. I couldn't balance a checkbook to save my life. We work well together. He handles the financing, and I do the marketing and sales.

Helping a seller out of a bad situation is really rewarding to me. The other day, we were working with a guy that was about to lose everything, and we got him out of it with money in his pocket. He hugged us and sent me a beautiful note saying he's so grateful for me that he can't believe we were able to do this. We hear that over and over from sellers because we work with pre-foreclosures and probates. So many people are just stuck, and they don't know how to get out or what their options are.

So, it's personally rewarding, and I can't wait to wake up and go to work. I worked 30 years in the same thing, and I was just bored, and now I'm not. I'm excited, and I love what I do. Plus, this has changed things financially – it's a very lucrative industry.

On Being a Woman Investor

I direct mail, and I send about 3000 letters per month. I probably get 25 calls a week, and I hear over and over that they called me because I'm a woman.

Women are more compassionate, they have more empathy, and people trust women more than they trust men.

So, I think being a woman in this industry is a huge advantage.

On Work Life Balance

My husband and I have been married for 33 years. He has his own business, and I have my business.

We have good household help which is necessary because I work 24/7. My husband is understanding of the time commitment my work requires.

I have friends in this business that have children, and it's a challenge for them. They can't dive in head first because a lot of the meetings are at night and it may be difficult to attend if you've got little kids at home. Meetings with sellers are usually on nights and weekends, so your family needs to be supportive of your schedule.

Lessons Learned/ What I Wish I Knew

I wish that I hadn't invested so much money in training because I could have learned so much more from local REI groups. The investment community has taught me more than I ever learned with high-dollar real estate education services.

The basic nuts and bolts training is available anywhere. You can learn from online courses and YouTube videos. I believed that I needed to go to college and earn a Bachelor's degree in Real Estate. I didn't need that degree. I often said I that I needed to get a realtor's license, but I don't need the license.

I also wish I would have known that it takes a long time to make money in this business. You're going to make money, but you've got to work really, really hard and you've got to have access to capital. You've probably heard it a lot – use other people's money.

Be persistent and dedicated, and never give up. Most people that I know in real estate investing say it takes at least two years to get there.

Words of Wisdom

Start educating yourself by listening to podcasts while you're driving. I listen to *BiggerPockets Real Estate* and *Flipping Junkie* podcasts every day. There are several others you can listen to also. Watch YouTube videos on real estate and go to local REI clubs to network.

Have realistic expectations. This is a lifetime career, and it doesn't happen overnight. Give yourself a year before you even get a deal. You're going to be knocking on doors. You're going to be falling and failing. Just keep going.

If I Could Give Advice to My Newbie Investor Self

I would tell my newbie investor self to be prepared to work 24/7, give 150 percent, don't ever give up, and you'll be successful. I mentor a lot of new investors, and I talk them out of quitting. If you want it bad enough, you can do it.

Know that it's not anything like the get rich quick you see on HGTV. It's a lot of work, and the rewards come at the end. Keep going, be persistent and consistent, work hard, don't take no for an answer, and don't quit. And if you're on your 20th deal and people say no, keep going until you get your 21st. Stay focused with your goal in mind.

Contact Susan Tierney

Websites
S2Equities.com
CasaBellaTejas.com

MISSI LOU WILSON

MISSI LOU WILSON

Missi Lou Wilson is a native Texan who consistently goes above and beyond for her real estate clients utilizing marketing, social media, real estate trends, and forecasting.

She is considered a trusted resource for her clients because she is organized, dedicated, and always working for their best interests. Missi takes the time to interview her clients to understand their goals and makes sure to manage expectations properly.

Outside of her career, Missi is a proud mother and has a servant's heart to be involved in the communities in which she serves. Missi became a realtor to help people buy, sell, and invest in Texas Real Estate.

She develops a strategic action plan for pricing, staging, marketing and negotiating all the way to the close of sale. Missi's attention to detail, listening to her clients, and providing valuable feedback is instrumental in her success.

Beginning the Journey

I had a colorful childhood. My mom had a lot of bad things thrown at her, and it caused us to have a hell of a childhood. My grandfather burned our house down when I was ten. My mom just couldn't recover from that. She was a single mom, and we moved around a lot. I ended up at 14 different schools, so I was always the new girl at school, and being the new girl is not easy. You have to really go out of your way to make people like you.

I got good at being an entertainer and getting people's attention and trying to engage others so that I could eat in the lunchroom and not have to eat in the bathroom. I think that really helped prepare me for a lot of what I do today in networking and trying to gain business.

I worked full time. If I wasn't at school, I was cleaning churches. Once I was old enough to have a real job, I always had two jobs at a time. I graduated from high school early in my junior year. I bought a car with the money I had saved, and off to Lubbock I went for school.

How Real Estate Investing Changed My Life

Real estate changed it for the better. When I first got into the industry, I learned that there's a really good support system in the community. I have met some of my very best friends and major inspirations in my life just being in this field. I get to meet other realtors, lenders, inspectors, and people that are on so many different journeys.

I didn't realize that I could retain more and that my brain could open up and I could learn more at my age until I got into real estate. You have to put it first above anything else a lot of times. And not everybody's okay with that. Over 60 percent of realtors go through a divorce because of their job. My six-year relationship ended because I focused only on real estate when I first started.

As soon as I got my real estate license, I joined a program that gave a percentage of my commissions back to my clients if they served in the military, or were law enforcement or firefighters. I was active with many veteran programs in the area. I was speaking at an event for a program called 22 Kill, and Mark Warner, owner of KVGI radio, approached me about being a host and talking about real estate.

At first, I didn't want to do it because I was afraid of giving bad advice and I didn't want to get sued. Mark reassured me it would be fine, and being the risk taker that I am, I decided to do it. I've been doing my radio show, *MissInformed*, off and on for four years, and I love it. It's my favorite thing.

I get to talk about common misconceptions, small businesses, pillars of the community, and people that I meet and I really like or enjoy. I love finding people with the gift of gab. I can focus on charities and spotlight different charities out that don't get enough recognition or that need funding because they're trying to do something wonderful.

On Being a Woman Investor

Women are just different, and so we handle things differently. Women can multitask and often have to focus on our job and be the nurturer and the caregiver for the house at the same time.

When I first started, I would never meet somebody who I didn't know at a property without first meeting them at my office. If they didn't want to meet at my office, that was a red flag.

Sometimes a client will hit on you when showing a house. Once, a husband hit on me when his wife wasn't in the room. I've had lenders and contractors that have made me feel uncomfortable. For me, the best strategy has been to assume that every guy is interested and act accordingly. I make sure I have boundaries up. I'm polite, but I am distant, and I try to make sure that I don't do anything that's going to sway them.

I enjoy making people laugh and smile, and that can sometimes be misconstrued as flirting. So, I have to hold back and make sure that I'm careful with how I speak and cautious with my body language.

On Work Life Balance

I struggle with this daily. I'm kind of a workhorse because I've been working since such a young age. Working is all I really do so I'm reminded often by those around me to take breaks.

One of the things that I would recommend is trying to be present and dedicate specific time as family time. I set appointments with my family. If you try to reach me on a Thursday night and I don't answer, it's because I'm with my nine-year-old and we're at a movie, or working on a project, or doing something fun. Making an appointment with your family may sound silly, but it helps you maintain that work/life balance.

Lessons Learned/ What I Wish I Knew

I wish that I had known hard it was going to be because I was not prepared for many of the different things that came at me. I can be naive. I love people a little too much, and I think that one of the reasons I'm successful is I genuinely enjoy people and different personalities.

In this industry, just like there are so many fun and awesome people, there are also a lot of people that want to take advantage of you. I wasted my time helping a lot of people that weren't necessarily grateful as I would've hoped.

Words of Wisdom

Education is key and be prepared to starve your first year. I can't tell you how hard it is when I'm on the other end of a deal and the other realtor doesn't understand what is happening.

Pay for that education, pay attention, and get the reading done. Don't stop with just the minimum requirements. Continue your education, find things in the field that interest you, and sharpen your skills with that. The more you know, the more people will start looking to you, and you'll be able to ultimately gain more business.

If I Could Give Advice to My Newbie Investor Self

Don't be scared. Do whatever you want to do. Just go for it and stop wasting time. Make the jump, get your own brokerage, make the job change, and go work for that different person that you want to work for. Don't be scared.

Contact Missi Lou Wilson

Business
Northbrook Realty Group

Email
missilwilson@gmail.com

Phone
254-722-3361

Website
NorthbrookRealtyGroup.com

Facebook
Facebook.com/MissiLou100

LinkedIn
Linkedin.com/in/Missi-Wilson

YouTube
YouTube.com/channel/UC4DemabKx7yhNReQ8mesvGw

Instagram
@MissInformedTexas

SHENOAH GROVE

SHENOAH GROVE

Shenoah Grove owns and operates the Dallas REIA with her husband, Phill Grove. She's been operating the Texas Wealth Network since 2002 and has seen it grow over the years, in up markets and down markets.

Shenoah has been investing in real estate since 2003. She holds a B.A. from the University of Texas and an M.B.A. from Rice University. She's also a REALTOR and Broker licensed in Texas.

Shenoah is a well-known local investor and national speaker with tens of thousands of customers and followers nationwide and around the world. She has a no-B.S. approach to investing and teaching.

At any time, Shenoah and Phill typically hold title to 20+ residential rental or fix and flip properties in central Texas. They live in Barton Creek with their son, Zilker.

Beginning the Journey

I'm a fourth-generation real estate investor. My great grandparents owned about 18 properties. My grandmother owned about 10. My mom and my stepfather own about 12. My mom tried to get me into real estate investing when I was in college, but I wanted to do the corporate America thing because I thought there was more money in that.

While I was working in corporate America at a job that was taking up all my time, my mom was getting rich off her real estate investments.

I started investing in 2003 and left my full-time job in 2004 to invest in real estate full time. From the beginning, I was active in real estate investor associations and influential in the leadership of those associations.

After years of successful investing and helping others, I eventually took over the real estate investing association that I had been volunteering with and started several other organizations around Texas.

How Real Estate Investing Changed My Life

My significant other, Phill, and I have several things in common, and we are both what we call long-term greedy. We always wanted to build wealth and be comfortable if we ever decide to retire.

Sometimes you have to make sacrifices to build out that wealth and security. We made many sacrifices early on by exchanging short-term income for long-term wealth. I always joke that Phill and I have the Blue Bell Ice Cream investing strategy and philosophy: we eat all we can, and we sell the rest.

For us, that means we keep as many rental properties as we can to build our wealth and retirement savings, and we sell enough to fund our lifestyle, pay the bills, and enjoy life. That's what has built out a lot of our wealth, and the truth is, it takes time.

Early in our investing, there were times where we didn't have a lot of money in the bank account, but we knew to not just look at our bank account, but also look at our balance sheet.

Assets minus liabilities was something that really allowed us to be where we are today. There were some sacrifices involved, but if I had to do it all over again, I would do the exact same thing. I joked that there were times as real estate investors we were eating Ramen noodles so that we could eat steak later.

There's a saying that if for the next five years you will do what no one else will do, then for the rest of your life, you can live like no one else can live. And that's something we certainly very much took to heart in our investing to feel comfortable with our investments.

When we first started investing, we were looking for the ability to replace our income, build our wealth, and get wealth from our homestead investing, too. We didn't concern ourselves with how much money was in the bank but instead focused on how much we were able to keep in terms of the properties and the assets.

I believe the most powerful force in the universe is compound interest. Specifically, the more assets that you have that are compounding interest on each other. For us, that was rental properties. The more availability and the more ability you'll have to build that wealth and build that level of comfort and live that life that most people cannot live.

It's just like saving in a 401k. You're able to put a certain percentage of your income away into that 401k. Do you make a sacrifice to do that? Yes, you do. You may not drive a fancy car or live in the biggest house, but you're saving for your future. So ultimately, you're putting yourself in the best position, although it may not feel that way at the moment.

You can't look at what everybody else is doing. They could be taking short-term wins, or it could be something else. In ten years, they may not look as good as you on paper. You must suspend that comparison to others and feel comfortable making some of those different sacrifices so that you can have a life of abundance down the road. There is a happy medium, but for us, we pushed it to the extreme to build wealth as early on as possible because we wanted that compounding.

And the beauty of real estate is that it's a leveraged asset if you're not buying with all cash. That leverage is what allows you to buy not just one $200,000 house with cash, but to buy maybe ten $200,000 houses for $20,000 apiece. Then you get the appreciation on the full value, which is $200,000 for each of those ten houses. That's what we were looking for. Combined with the principal pay down that the tenants are helping with, that has landed us on top.

On Being a Woman Investor

In many cases, men prefer to do business with men. Women don't necessarily prefer only doing business with other women but are definitely more open to working with women than men are. Real estate investing is a male-dominated industry, but the way that I see it and what I tell other female investors is find out what your assets are and leverage those assets.

The one big advantage that I feel like women have over men is women often tend to get more into helping and the service side of it. I don't want to stereotype because I don't think that's fair or 100 percent accurate, but it just seems like the women are a little bit more caring.

Sometimes we're buying houses from people in serious financial trouble. That extra love and care is sometimes the difference maker. So, from that perspective, I can see women having a much greater bond that will ultimately seal the deal.

One disadvantage I see that women have over men is sometimes women are reluctant to be forceful with a homeowner in a dire situation. This ultimately is a disservice to a homeowner that is about to go to foreclosure. Sometimes I see women say, "Well, I told them, but they didn't do anything." You need to be able to communicate effectively and encourage people to move forward quickly to save themselves from what could be a very difficult situation if they allow the house to go into foreclosure.

Being successful or unsuccessful on a project has nothing to do with gender; it's all about the scope of work. If you are detailed in your scope of work when you first set up the renovation project and budget, your odds for success and having a good outcome are 100 percent higher than if you don't have a good scope of work. Make sure the scope of work is outlined in writing. If contractors have agreed to that scope of work in writing, they have an obligation to complete the work.

I've had to scream and yell to get work finished and get it finished correctly. Don't be afraid to call out poor workmanship. And I think the most important thing, again, is that initial scope of work and set a precedent early on what is acceptable and what is not.

Take that responsibility very seriously and protect yourself. I'll introduce myself to a contractor as "No Change Orders Shenoah." So, let's make sure when we go through the scope of work together, I'm not setting myself up, and you're not setting yourself or me up to come back and have a conversation of we missed this, this is what we're going to have to add or change. I want to consider everything now so that I don't have to go back and reset expectations, reset a budget, reset work orders, slide on my project, or anything like that.

I will spend two to four hours to write the scope of a project. That's a long time. In the past, when I have not thoroughly set up the initial scope of work, it has cost me money.

On Work-Life Balance

Over the years, I have tried to eliminate as many minimum-wage activities as possible so that I can focus on the activities that bring me the highest return on my investment and the highest return on my time. I could wash all my dishes and do all my laundry, cleaning, and cooking, but I'm not going to get further in my ability to build wealth while doing that.

I am obsessed about my business, my family, and my fitness, and I have figured out how to have all those things. I live a very different life than probably most people, and most real estate investors, but I've found I am able to be obsessed and be balanced at the same time on the things that are most important to me and the things that are part of my ultimate purpose.

As Americans, we all have a very deep, puritan work ethic, and a lot of that comes from spending time with our grandparents who went through the Great Depression, and then with our parents who were also very hard workers.

Phill and I always say we can't teach hard work, but that work ethic is essential. Understand the things that got you there are also going to be the things that hold you there. The things that got you to a salary of $100,000 a year are going to be different than the things that will get you to a salary of $500,000 a year. What got you to $500,000 is going to be different than things that get you to a $1,000,000 or $10,000,000.

But those things are probably also the things that are holding you back, which is the desire to do everything yourself. Phill and I are continually looking for things that we should we not be doing, and ways to create a process around these things. Can we hire someone else to do it so that we can have the three things that are most important to us: family, business, health and fitness? We have a driver to that helps us in our business and makes us less stressed which gives us better health. We are able to do more things with our son than probably most people are able to, but we get to do it because of the lifestyle we created through real estate investing.

Don't hire someone to help you with these activities so you can go shopping. Hire someone to do these so you can focus on the most important things in your life, which may be spending time with family, spending time on your business, or spending time on your health and fitness. Free your time so that you can focus on building in a new and bigger direction.

Lessons Learned/ What I Wish I Knew

In our training, we have a presentation called *Get Rich Slow* that shows you how to build wealth being a landlord. When we first started investing, we looked for cash flow and properties. But we figured out a few years in that the cash flow really doesn't matter. What matters is the appreciation because it's appreciating on the total value of that property.

So, if we would have purchased better properties in better areas, then our portfolio might be 20-30 percent more than it is today. But we spent some of our early money buying rental properties that were only cash flowing and not appreciating. As a real estate investor, everyone wants cash flow, and everyone wants appreciation. Pick one. Usually, the houses that have the best cash flow have less appreciation.

I hear some investors say that they get a thousand dollars a month cash flow. Those investors must have paid cash for those properties. So, they only have one house instead of having 21. I would rather have 21 houses to have leverage. I'm not saying 100 percent debt leverage. I'm saying be smart about your leverage, and use that to your advantage to get more compound interest on more assets. If we were to do it again, in our first three to five years, we would buy more appreciating rental properties than cash flow properties.

The discount you get on houses that appreciate quickly doesn't matter. If you are buying, fixing and flipping, the discount is all that matters. You've got to get it at 70 percent of ARV minus repairs. At first, we applied that 70 percent of ARV minus repairs formula to all properties whether we were buying and fixing and flipping or buying and holding.

With that mindset, we left properties that were appreciating rapidly, and we didn't go after them for rental properties because we didn't get the right initial price. There are properties that we sold that we should not have sold because we didn't put those things together.

Now I don't care about the cash flow; I can generate cash flow by doing a wholesale, a fix and flip, a short sale, etc. I have a lot of different strategies that generate an income for me.

After I reach a certain amount of income, I want to generate wealth, so I need to be buying the right properties.

Words of Wisdom

Do not pay for services that are not 100 percent complete. If you do it once, you've set the precedent that you will pay before the job is complete. Then, you will end up with a project with ten things half done, and you've got an issue with your contractor. You can't get them to come back to finish those ten half-done things. You need to understand how a contractor thinks.

Realize that no one's going to spend your money like you are, and no one is going to save your money like you are.

Take dramatic action. Get out of your comfort zone. You may have some uncomfortable conversations with people who are about to lose their homes. Raise the stakes and get in their face and take ownership of it. One of the things that I say to a lot of investors is if this person goes to foreclosure and you talked to him, their foreclosure is on you because you did not do enough. And I hope you sleep well tonight thinking about that.

Consistently be marketing and networking. There's just no stopping that. One of the most successful and well-known companies in the world, Coca Cola, advertises every minute of every hour of every day in every language in every country. What do you think you should do for your little bitty old brand?

If I Could Give Advice to My Newbie Investor Self

Don't pass up appreciating properties for cash flow properties.

Contact Shenoah Grove

Business
Texas Wealth Network

Website
TexasWealthNetwork.com

Facebook
Facebook.com/DallasREIA

Phone
512-853-9522

BELKIS GUIFARRO

BELKIS GUIFARRO

Belkis Guifarro is a mother, entrepreneur, a strong woman, and loves life! She was born in Honduras and came to the United States as a child.

Belkis was a quick learner, and after high school, she attended the University of Texas at Austin. She worked in the corporate world for a few years only to realize she didn't want to do that for the rest of her life.

In May 2016, Belkis and her husband began learning how to invest in real estate. They started their own real estate investing company, and quickly replaced their old jobs.

Belkis enjoys spending the days with her daughters at the zoo or museums hoping they learn as much as they can and develop to become strong women themselves.

She enjoys helping other people get out of difficult situations, investing in real estate, and teaching others to find financial freedom for themselves!

Beginning the Journey

I was working fulltime in Human Resources as a recruiter, and I was spending a lot of time at work. I had a toddler and a baby at home. I was ready for a change, and I wanted to spend more time with my girls. I knew that I needed to become the owner of my own time instead of my time belonging to a company.

So, I researched different opportunities on the Internet and found a real estate association. My husband, Erick, and I decided to check it out. We learned a few things there. Then, we decided to make real estate investing a full-time job.

We really didn't know what we were getting into. The only real estate experience we had was when we purchased our house. So, we knew we needed to educate ourselves. We spent about two thousand dollars on training and started from there. Every day we would try new marketing techniques to get better at whatever we were doing.

How Real Estate Investing Changed My Life

It's been an awesome journey. Before starting in real estate investing, we didn't have a plan of where we were going or how we were going to do things. Now, we're in control of our time. I get to spend a lot of time with my daughters and can watch them grow.

Before we started this business, our net worth was less than $300,000. Within six months of starting this journey, we had over a million dollars in assets plus whatever cash we were making at the time.

We owned our house and were saving money, but we were also spending money on dumb things. We weren't educated on how to invest, didn't know how to invest in ourselves, and didn't realize that investing in yourself is the best investment that you can make.

Within six months, we went from not only saving but investing in multi-family homes. We got our first few rentals. Then, we had our first few new construction projects.

Now, my daughters say they want to own a hotel. That was something they would have never considered before because they weren't exposed to anything like that. Because of our job and what we do, they think the world is theirs, and they can buy everything and anything they want. Real estate investing has been a life-changing experience for my entire family.

On Being a Woman Investor

I started investing young, and I look younger than I am. Many people thought I was still in high school and it was a little difficult for others to take me seriously. People didn't know whether I knew what I was talking about. I had those challenges, but I didn't take it personally. I decided that I was going to do the best that I could with myself and prove that I was someone to be taken seriously.

I didn't focus on the outside people. I focused more on my business and helping the people in my business. I feel that for me to get where I want to be, I need to help as many people as I can get to where they want to be.

Soon people who initially saw me as somebody that couldn't do well in this business now saw me as somebody that could get things done. Other investors would seek my advice when they needed help. They could count on me to help them close deals the way that I was closing deals.

There are challenges and shying away from those challenges is not going to help you grow. Confronting those challenges head-on will make you grow and be successful. It doesn't matter what other people say or how they view you; it's about how you look at yourself and what you do that's going to help you move forward.

On Work Life Balance

My home life is very much part of my real estate investing career. When my husband and I started the business, we had two little ones. My youngest was about two and a half years old. In this business, you can't always schedule everything. You want to plan and schedule everything so you can be as productive as possible with your day, but it doesn't always work out.

I worked with a lot of foreclosures and buyers or sellers sometimes want to see a property NOW. There's no time to call a babysitter or drop off my kids with someone. You have to stop everything and take your two-and-a-half-year-old with you to get the contract right then.

My kids know about our business, and they enjoy helping make decisions when we're doing fix and flips. My six-year-old daughter will walk through a property and say, "I want this room to be pink." She likes to pick out finishes for the tile and backsplash. So, in a way, I've incorporated my personal life into my business life because I spend a lot of time with my kids.

They go to school now, and I try to do as much work as possible while they're in school. I spend as much time with them as I can after school. If that means they have to go to an appointment with me, then they do that. If I need to go to the store to pick out some finishes, we go together. We're always spending time together, so my personal life has merged with my business life.

Lessons Learned/ What I Wish I Knew

One of the first mistakes we made was wondering whether we would have enough money. We got caught up thinking *I'm going to get the contract, but where am I going to get the money?* The money comes; it's not a problem.

Also, don't take things personally. When we first started dealing with foreclosures, I would take on the seller's problems. It caused me a lot of grief, sadness, and stress. At one point, I ended up in the hospital because of all the things that were going on. I learned I could solve other's problems without carrying it around which allowed me to serve people without causing myself stress.

For example, we were working with a single mother who had a daughter in high school and was losing her house due to foreclosure. Not only that, she couldn't pay her bills and had no running water or electricity. I have two little girls, and it upset me to think about this child getting up every morning and going to school without being able to take a shower because there's no running water. My immediate thought was to buy the house and to pay for their utilities.

We connected the electricity and the water. But then any time I would call the owner to get some paperwork done or ask about the house, she would cry and tell me about other problems that she was having. The only way I knew how to solve that was to give her more money.

Her situation was causing her so much stress that her hair was falling out. She was so upset and distracted when she went to work that they sent her home without pay. She said they didn't have any food and it broke my heart to hear her say that. I immediately went to the grocery store, bought them some food, and brought it to them.

She was also too distraught to be looking for a new home, so I was the one going out to look at possible rentals. The pressure built up and I remember one night that I just started to cry. My husband said to stop because I was already doing more than enough to help them.

It was frustrating that she didn't try to reciprocate what I was doing for her. I wanted her to get up and do it with me for her daughter. I tried to encourage this young lady as she was going out into the world and let her see that when times are tough, there's always someone or something that's going to make your life go forward and move forward. And your job is to learn from the mistakes and to grow from them and keep going forward.

They sold their house and moved into a rental home with some money in their pockets. The mom started a credit repair company after seeing how she was able to save her credit from being tarnished by foreclosure, and she wanted to help others in a similar situation.

Words of Wisdom

Focus on your marketing. Acquiring leads is a very big part of this business. Even if it takes a year or if it only takes a couple of months, you have to focus on that. Don't take your foot off the pedal when it comes to marketing.

You're not only marketing for sellers; you're also marketing for buyers because guess what? If you get a contract and you need to convert, you must have someone to buy the property from you.

I would recommend always growing your buyer's list. Add to it as often as you can because you can never have enough buyers. If you market for buyers and sellers, you can expect to be successful. You can't only market to one or the other; you have to do both.

If I Could Give Advice to My Newbie Investor Self

Enjoy the little things and reward yourself. It's a great way to keep yourself motivated in this business, and you have to be self-motivated in this business to be able to move forward. Otherwise, it's very easy to want to quit.

Read books and take an active role in every process. There will come a time when everything is outsourced because you have so many things going on and you won't get to make certain decisions.

At first, we poured every single dime that we were making as profit back into the business. Instead of putting it all back into your business, take some of the profits and enjoy yourself because that's why you're doing this – you want to have a comfortable lifestyle, and you want to be able to do certain things.

So why not do them now when you are making money? Your business will continue to grow, so start living the life now instead of saying, "I'm going to work hard for x amount of years and then I'm going to live this lavish lifestyle."

That's what I would tell myself because at first, we focused so much on acquiring properties and making sure every dime went back and went back and went back that we made ourselves super cash poor. Then we weren't able to enjoy things, and we were worried about other stuff that we shouldn't have been worried about.

Contact Belkis Guifarro

Business
WBT Partners, LLC & Latino REIA Houston

Email
Belkis@wbtpartners.com

Phone
281-848-8006

Website
LatinoREIAHouston.com

Facebook
Facebook.com/Belkis.Guifarro

LinkedIn
LinkedIn.com/in/Belkis-Guifarro

Twitter
Twitter.com/REIBelkis

Instagram
Instagram.com/BelkisGuif
Instagram.com/LatinoREIAHouston

Made in the
USA
Lexington, KY